KINGFISHER READERS

Tadpoles and Frogs

Thea Feldman

KINGFISHER

NEW YORK

KINGFISHER
LONDON & NEW YORK

Copyright © Kingfisher 2013
Published in the United States and Canada by Kingfisher,
175 Fifth Ave., New York, NY 10010
Kingfisher is an imprint of Macmillan Children's Books, London.
All rights reserved.

Distributed in the U.S. by Macmillan,
175 Fifth Ave., New York, NY 10010

Library of Congress Cataloging-in-Publication data
has been applied for.

Series editor: Thea Feldman
Literacy consultant: Ellie Costa, Bank Street College, New York

ISBN: 978-0-7534-7086-2 (HB)
ISBN: 978-0-7534-7087-9 (PB)

Kingfisher books are available for special promotions
and premiums. For details contact: Special Markets
Department, Macmillan, 175 Fifth Ave.,
New York, NY 10010.

For more information, please visit
www.kingfisherbooks.com

Printed in China
9 8 7 6 5 4 3 2 1
1TR/0713/WKT/UG/115MA

Picture credits
The Publisher would like to thank the following for permission to reproduce their
material. Every care has been taken to trace copyright holders. However, if there have
been unintentional omissions or failure to trace copyright holders, we apologize and
will, if informed, endeavor to make corrections in any future edition.

Top = t; Bottom = b; Center = c; Left = l; Right = r

Cover Shutterstock/worldswildlifewonders; Pages 3 Frank Lane Picture Agency (FLPA)/Scott
Leslie/Minden Pictures; 4–5 FLPA/Andrew Bailey; 5t Shutterstock/ivaskes; 6–7 FLPA/David
Tipling; 8–9 FLPA/Richard Becker; 9t FLPA/Jean Hall; 10 Superstock/Juniors; 11 FLPA/Larry
West; 12 Superstock/NaturePL; 13 FLPA/S & D & K Maslowski; 14 FLPA/Andrew Bailey; 15t
FLPA/Dave Pressland; 15b FLPA/Thomas Marent/Minden Pictures; 16 Superstock/NaturePL;
17 Shutterstock/Tom Reichner; 18–19 FLPA/Thomas Marent/Minden Pictures; 20–21 naturepl.
com/Thomas Lazar; 22–23 Getty/Oktay Ortakcioglu; 23t FLPA/Rene Krekels/FN/Minden;
24t Shutterstock/Alfredo Maiquez; 24b Shutterstock/Dirk Ercken; 25t Shutterstock/Cathy
Keifer; 25b FLPA/Rene Krekels/FN/Minden; 26 Shutterstock/worldswildlifewonders; 27
FLPA/Christian Ziegler/Minden Pictures; 28 NHPA/Photoshot/Ant; 29 FLPA/Denis Palanque/
Biosphoto; 30t FLPA/Michael Dietrich/Imagebroker; 30b Shutterstock/Ryan M. Bolton;
31t FLPA/Thomas Marent/Minden Pictures; 31b FLPA/Scott Leslie/Minden Pictures.

It is spring.

Frogs come to the pond.

Why?

They lay eggs in the water!

A frog lays many eggs.

Then she leaves
the pond.

Let's look at the eggs.

They are not hard like
bird eggs.

They are soft like jelly.

There is something dark
inside each one.

What is it?

It is a baby frog!

The frog grows and grows inside the egg.

One day it wiggles out.

Hello, baby frog!

The baby frog is called
a **tadpole**.

A tadpole has a long tail.

It breathes with **gills**.

gills

You can see the gills.

The tadpole does not look like a grown-up frog.

Tadpoles start to swim
as soon as they are born.

They swim to find
plants to eat.

They swim away from
bigger, hungry animals.

A tadpole changes as it grows.

Look!

Now it has tiny legs.

There is skin between
each toe.

The tadpole grows
two more legs.

When it is about three
months old, a tadpole
becomes a **froglet**.

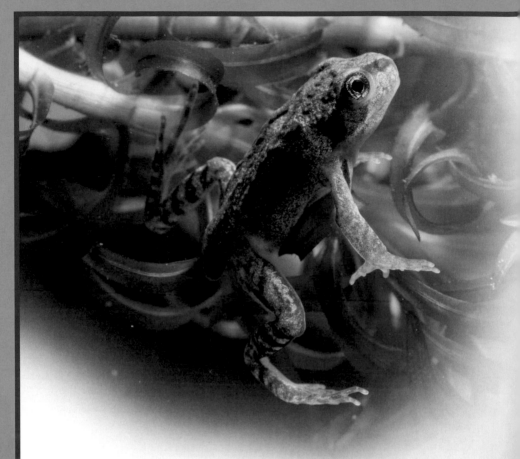

A froglet changes as it grows.

Its arms and legs get longer.

It loses its tail.

Its gills go inside its body.

After about one month,
the froglet becomes a
grown-up frog!

Hop! A frog hops on land.

It uses its long back legs.

On land a frog
uses **lungs** to breathe.

In water it uses
gills to breathe.

Gulp!

A frog catches insects
with its long, sticky tongue.

Croak!

A frog calls out
to find other frogs.

There are thousands of
different kinds of frogs.

Toads are a lot like frogs.

Toads have bumpy skin.

Some frogs lay
eggs in trees.

When the eggs **hatch**
the tadpoles fall into
the water!

They grow up in the water.

Some frogs lay eggs underground.

When this frog's eggs hatch they are already froglets!

Some frogs and toads carry
their eggs.

This male toad carries
the eggs of a female toad
on his back legs!

Frogs lay eggs in water.

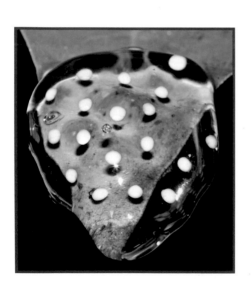

They lay
them in trees.

They even carry eggs.

Wherever there are frog eggs,
it means new frogs are on
the way!

Glossary

froglet a young frog that is older than a tadpole

gills parts of the body that tadpoles and frogs use to breathe air when they are in water. Gills are on the outside of a tadpole's body and on the inside of a frog's body.

hatch to break out of an egg and be born

lungs parts inside an animal's body that are used to breathe air

tadpole a baby frog